SMOKING MEAT

Ultimate Smoker Cookbook for **Real Barbecue** **The Art of Smoking Meat** for Real Pitmasters

By Gary Mercer

Table of Contents

INTRODUCTION

The ultimate how-to guide for smoking all types of meat, poultry, and game. This book on smoking meats for beginners is the guide to mastering the low and slow art of smoking beef, lamb, poultry, pork and game at your home. This guide is an essential book for beginners who want to smoke meat without needing expert help from others. This book offers detailed guidance obtained by years of smoking meat, includes clear instructions and step-by-step directions for every recipe. This is the only guide you will ever need to professionally smoke a variety of meat. From well-known beef brisket, ribeye, the book includes delicate lamb, turkey, venison, chicken, and pheasant smoked meat recipes. The book includes full-color photographs of every finished meal to make your job easier. Whether you are a beginner meat smoker or looking to go beyond the basics, the book gives you the tools and tips you need to start that perfectly smoked meat.

WHY SMOKING

Smoking is generally used as one of the cooking methods now days. The food enrich in protein such as meat would spoil quickly, if cooked for a longer period of time with modern cooking techniques. Whereas, Smoking is a low & slow process of cooking the meat. Where there is a smoke, there is a flavor. With white smoke, you can boost the flavor of your food. In addition to this statement, you can preserve the nutrition present inside the food as well. This is flexible & one of the oldest techniques of making food. It's essential for you to brush the marinade over your food while you cook and let the miracle happen. The only thing you need to do is to add a handful of fresh coals or wood chips as and when required. Just taste your regular grilled meat and a smoked meat, you yourself would find the difference. Remember one thing i.e. "Smoking is an art". With a little time & practice even you can become an expert. Once you become an expert with smoking technique, believe me you would never look for other cooking techniques. To find one which smoking technique works for you, you must experiment with different woods & cooking methods. Just cook the meat over indirect heat source & cook it for hours. When smoking your meats, it's very important that you let the smoke to escape & move around.

CHAPTER 1
SMOKING TIPS
AND TRICKS

Before starting the recipes, let's discuss a few tips and tricks about smoking meats.

SELECTING A SMOKER

You need to invest in a good smoker if you are going to smoke meat on a regular basis. Consider these options when buying a smoker. Here are two natural fire option for you:

- Charcoal smokers are fueled with a combination of charcoal and wood. Charcoal burns easily and the temperature remains steady, so you won't have any problem with a charcoal smoker. The wood gives a great flavor to the meat and you will enjoy smoking meats.

- Wood smoker: The wood smoker will give your brisket and ribs the best smoky flavor and taste, but it is a bit harder to cook with wood. Both hardwood blocks and chips are used as fuel.

Choose your wood

You need to choose your wood carefully because the type of wood you will use affect greatly to the flavor and taste of the meat. Here are a few options for you:

- Maple: Maple has a smoky and sweet taste and goes well with pork or poultry

- Alder: Alder is sweet and light. Perfect for poultry and fish.

- Apple: Apple has a mild and sweet flavor. Goes well with pork, fish, and poultry.

- Oak: Oak is great for slow cooking. Ideal for game, pork, beef, and lamb.

- Mesquite: Mesquite has a smoky flavor and extremely strong. Goes well with pork or beef.

- Hickory: Has a smoky and strong flavor. Goes well with beef and lamb.

- Cherry Has a mild and sweet flavor. Great for pork, beef, and turkey

To cook the meat, you may refer the below mentioned chart that can help you with selecting the best wood chips/chunks

Wood Type	Lamb	Chicken	Beef	Pork
Apple	Yes	Yes	No	No
Alder	Yes	Yes	No	Yes
Cherry	Yes	Yes	Yes	Yes
Hickory	No	No	Yes	Yes
Maple	No	Yes	No	No
Mulberry	Yes	Yes	No	Yes
Mesquite	No	No	Yes	Yes
Oak	Yes	Yes	Yes	Yes
Pecan	No	Yes	Yes	Yes
Pear	No	Yes	No	Yes
Peach	No	Yes	No	Yes
Walnut	No	No	Yes	Yes

Remember, black smoke is bad and white smoke is good. Ensue proper ventilation for great tasting smoked meat.

SELECT THE RIGHT MEAT

Some meats are just ideal for the smoking process, including:

- Chicken

- Turkey

- Pork roast

- Ham

- Brisket

- Pork and beef ribs

- Corned beef

FIND THE RIGHT TEMPERATURE

- Start at 250F (120C): Start your smoker a bit hot. This extra heat gets the smoking process going.

- Temperature drop: Once you add the meat to the smoker, the temperature will drop, which is fine.

- Maintain the temperature. Monitor and maintain the temperature. Keep the temperature steady during the smoking process.

Avoid peeking every now and then. Smoke and heat two most important element makes your meat taste great. If you open the cover every now and then you lose both of them and your meat lose flavor. Only the lid only when you truly need it.

CHAPTER 2 BEEF
BRISKET

(TOTAL COOK TIME 22 HOURS TO 25 HOURS)

INGREDIENTS FOR 14 SERVINGS

- Brisket - 1 (13 –lb , 6 -kg)

The Rub

- Kosher salt – 1 cup
- Cracked black pepper – 1 cup
- Granulated sugar – 1 cup
- Paprika – ¼ cup
- Cumin – ¼ cup
- Onion powder – 1 tbsp.
- Garlic powder – 1 tbsp.
- Cayenne pepper – 1 tbsp.

The Fire

- Light your pit fire 1 hour prior to smoking
- Add wood 30 minutes prior to smoking

Method

1. In a bowl, combine cayenne pepper, garlic powder, onion powder, cumin, paprika, sugar, cracked black pepper, and kosher salt.

2. Apply a generous amount of rub to all sides of the brisket.

3. Place it in a pan and keep in the refrigerator overnight, uncovered.

4. Remove brisket from the refrigerator and allow to come to room temperature before placing it into the pit.

5. Make sure the pit temperature is 240F (115C) and place the brisket on the middle rack of the pit with tongs, fat cap facing up.

6. Maintain an even 240F (115C) temperature and don't allow fluctuation of more than 5 to 7 degrees throughout the cooking process.

7. Insert an instant read thermometer in the middle of the brisket after 8 hours. The target temperature is 175F (80 C).

8. The brisket will reach 175F after 4 to 6 more hours of cooking. Remove from the pit and allow to rest before slicing.

9. Slice and serve.

Beef Short Ribs

(Total cook time 10 hours to 11 hours)

Ingredients 4 servings

- Rack beef short plate ribs - 1 (4.5- to 6-lb.; 2 to 2.7kg)

The Fire

- Light your pit fire 1 hour prior to smoking
- Add wood 30 minutes prior to smoking

The Rub

- Kosher salt – 1 cup

- Cracked black pepper – 1 cup

Method

1. Generously season rib rack with black pepper and kosher salt.

2. Let the rib rest at room temperature for 1 hour, uncovered.

3. Stabilize pit temperature at 240F (115C) and place rib rack into the middle of the pit, meat side up.

4. Insert an instant-read thermometer in the middle after 6 hours. The target temperature is 195F (90C).

5. After 2 to 3 hours, the rib will react the target temperature.

6. Remove from the pit and rest for an hour before slicing.

7. Slice and serve.

Tenderloin

(total cook time 45 minutes to 1 hour)

Ingredients for 8 servings

The Meat

- Whole tenderloin – 1 (3.5- to 4,5-lb.; 1.6 to 2kg) silver skin removed

The Fire

- Light your pit fire 1 hour prior to smoking

- Add wood 30 minutes prior to smoking

The Rub

- Butcher's grind black pepper – 1 tsp.

- Kosher salt – ½ tsp.

- Garlic powder – ½ tsp.

- Onion powder – ½ tsp.

Method

1. In a bowl, mix the rub ingredients and rub the tenderloin evenly. Reserve a small amount of seasoning.

2. Allow the tenderloin to rest for an hour, uncovered.

3. Stabilize the pit temperature at 250F (120C). Place the tenderloin in the middle of the pit with tongs. Keep but end facing the heat source.

4. Insert an instant-read thermometer in the center after 45 minutes. The target temperature is 140F (60C) for medium rare and 160F (70C) for medium.

5. Once the meat reaches your desired temperate, remove it from the pit.

6. Rest for 10 minutes before slicing.

7. Slice and serve.

RIBEYE

(TOTAL COOK TIME 2 HOURS 18
MINUTES TO 2 HOURS 23 MINUTES)

INGREDIENTS FOR 4 SERVINGS

The Meat

- Ribeye steaks – 4 thick cuts (1 ¼ lb. (566g) each)

The Fire

- Light your pit fire 1 hour prior to smoking

- Add wood 30 minutes prior to smoking

The Rub

- Kosher salt – 1 cup

- Cracked black pepper – 1 cup

Method

1. Place steaks on a shallow tray and season liberally with salt and black pepper.

2. In the bottom of the tray, roll edges of steaks to cover with any remaining seasoning. Allow resting for an hour.

3. Stabilize the pit temperature at 235F (112C) and place the ribeye steaks into the middle of the pit with tongs. Make sure there is enough room between them.

4. Insert an instant read thermometer after 25 minutes into the middle of each steak to check. Remove the steaks once they reach

your desired temperature, after 3 to 10 more minutes.

5. In the coals in your firebox, create a flat spot with a shovel and place steaks directly on the coals. Sear both sides for 4 minutes total.

6. Allow resting the steaks for 10 minutes.

7. Then slice and serve.

SHOULDER

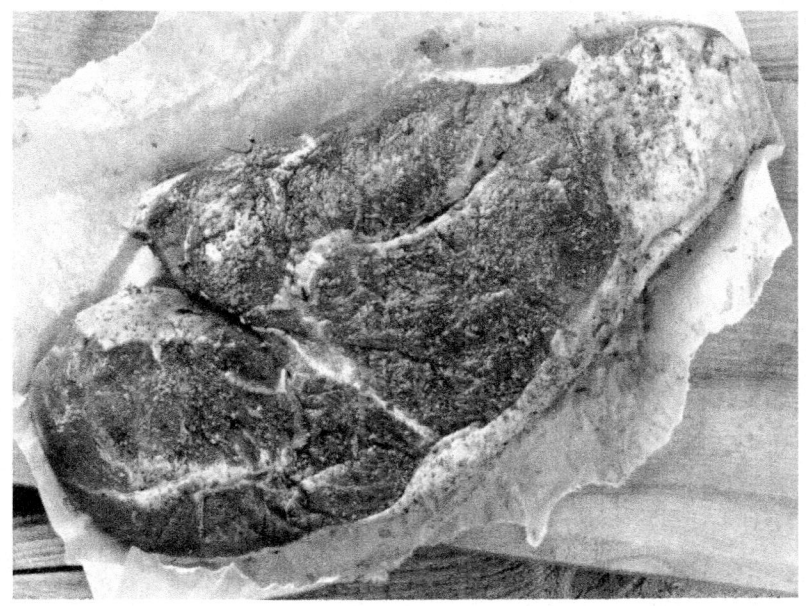

(TOTAL COOK TIME 18 TO 20 HOURS)

INGREDIENTS FOR 36 TO 40 SERVINGS

THE MEAT

- Untrimmed beef shoulder - 1 (16- to 22-lb.; 7 to 10kg)

The Fire

- Light your pit fire 1 hour prior to smoking

- Add wood 30 minutes prior to smoking

The Rub

- Kosher salt – 1 cup

- Cracked black pepper – 1 cup

- Granulated sugar – 1 cup

- Cayenne pepper – ½ tsp.

- Cumin – 1 tbsp.

- Garlic powder – 3 tbsp.

Method

1. In a bowl, mix all the rub ingredients.

2. Generously apply rub evenly to all surfaces of the shoulder. Place the meat on a large tray and keep in the refrigerator overnight, uncovered.

3. Remove from the refrigerator and 1 hour before placing in the pit.

4. Stabilize pit temperature at 250F(120C). place the clod in the middle of the pit, fat cap facing up and the thickest part facing the fire.

5. Insert an instant-read thermometer after 14 hours into the thickest part of the clod. The target temperature is 175F (79C).

6. After another 4 to 6 hours of cooking, clod will reach the desired temperature.

7. Remove from the pit and allow to rest for 1 hour.

8. Slice and serve.

Chapter 3 Lamb
Rack of Lamb

(TOTAL COOK TIME 45 MINUTES TO
1 HOUR 15 MINUTES)

INGREDIENTS FOR 4 SERVINGS

THE MEAT

- Racks of Lamb – 3, (2-lb.; 900g)

THE FIRE

- Light your pit fire 1 hour prior to smoking

- Add wood 30 minutes prior to smoking

THE RUB

- Kosher salt – ½ cup

- Cracked black pepper – ¼ cup

- Granulated sugar – 2 tbsp.

- Paprika – 2 tbsp.

- Cumin – 1 tbsp.

- Fresh rosemary – 1 sprig, finely chopped

- Fresh basil leaves – 6, coarsely chopped

METHOD

1. In a bowl, mix all the rub ingredients.

2. On each lamb rack, sprinkle an even coating of rub and gently pat surface with your hands to coat. Allow to rest 45 minutes at room temperature, uncovered.

3. Stabilize pit temperature at 270F (135C). Place the lamb racks in the middle of the pit with tongs; keep bones curved downward.

4. Use an instant-read thermometer to check the progress after 45 minutes. Don't touch

the bone with the probe. For medium rare the temperature is 145F (65C) and for medium, the temperature is 160F (70C).

5. Remove the racks when they are 5 degrees below your desired temperature, up to 30 more minutes.

6. Allow lamb racks to rest uncovered 25 minutes before slicing.

Lamb Shanks

(total cook time 3 hours 30 minutes)

Ingredients for 4 servings

The Meat

- Lamb shanks – 4, (1- lb.; 450g)

The Fire

- Light your pit fire 1 hour prior to smoking

- Add wood 30 minutes prior to smoking

The Rub

- Kosher salt – ½ cup

- Cracked black pepper – ¼ cup

- Granulated sugar – 2 tbsp.

- Garlic powder – 1 tbsp.

- Paprika – 1 tbsp.

- Cumin – 1 tbsp.

- Ground thyme – 2 tsp.

Method

1. Stabilize the pit temperature at 240F (115C). Place the lamb shanks in the middle of the pit with tongs. Make sure the larger ends face the heat.

2. With an instant-read thermometer, check each lamb shank after 2 hours, 30 minutes. Avoid the bones when checking. The target temperature is 160F (70C).

3. The lamb shanks will reach the target temperature after 1 hour.

4. Remove from the pit and rest uncovered for 30 minutes.

5. The meat should easily pull away from the bone. Serve.

LAMB NECKS

(TOTAL COOK TIME 5 HOURS 30 MINUTES TO 6 HOURS)

INGREDIENTS FOR 4 SERVINGS

- Lamb necks – 2 (5 -lb.; 2.3kg)

THE FIRE

- Light your pit fire 1 hour prior to smoking
- Add wood 30 minutes prior to smoking

THE RUB

- Kosher salt – ½ cup

- Cracked black pepper – ¼ cup

- Granulated sugar – 2 tbsp.

- Cumin – 2 tbsp.

- Paprika – 1 tbsp.

- Garlic powder – 1 tbsp.

- Cayenne pepper – 1 tsp.

METHOD

1. In a bowl, combine the rub ingredients and mix well.

2. Coat lamb necks evenly with rub and rest uncovered for at least 45 minutes.

3. Stabilize the pit temperature at 250F (120C). Place rack necks on the middle rack with tongs. Keep them away from any hot spots.

4. Insert an instant-read thermometer into the fattest part of each lamb neck after 4 hours and 30 minutes. The target temperature is 165F (75C).

5. After 1 to 1 hour 30 minutes later, lamb necks will reach the target temperature.

6. Remove from the pit and rest 35 minutes uncovered.

7. Slice and serve.

LAMB SHOULDER

(TOTAL COOK TIME 8 TO 9 HOURS)

INGREDIENTS FOR 10 SERVINGS

THE MEAT

- Lamb shoulder – 1 (4-6 lbs.; 1.8-2.7 kg) excess fat removed

The Fire

- Light your pit fire 1 hour prior to smoking

- Add wood 30 minutes prior to smoking

The Rub

- Sea salt – 2 ½ tbsp.

- Freshly ground black pepper – 1 ½ tbsp.

- Whole mustard seeds – 1 tbsp.

- Sweet paprika – 2 tbsp.

- Brown sugar – 1 ½ tbsp.

- Chopped rosemary leaves – 2 tbsp.

- Garlic – 4 cloves, crushed

- Mild American mustard – 4 tbsp.

Method

1. Except for the mustard, mix all the rub ingredients in a bowl.

2. Brush the lamb with mustard and cover with the rub mix.

3. Stabilize the pit temperature at 250F (120C). Place the meat with tongs in the middle of the pit.

4. The target temperature is 200F (93C). Cook for 8 hours then check with an instant read thermometer.

5. After 1 more hour of cooking the meat will be ready.

6. Remove from the pit. Rest for 30 minutes.

7. Slice and serve.

SMOKED LEG OF LAMB

(TOTAL COOK TIME 3 HOURS)

Ingredients for 4 servings

The Meat

- Boneless leg of lamb (2-2,5 lb; 900g- 1,2 kg) excess fat removed

The Fire

- Light your pit fire 1 hour prior to smoking

- Add wood 30 minutes prior to smoking

The Rub

- Garlic – 4 cloves, minced

- Salt – 2 tbsp.

- Fresh ground black pepper – 1 tbsp.

- Oregano – 2 tbsp.

- Thyme – 1 tsp.

- Olive oil – 2 tbsp.

Method

1. In a bowl, mix all the rub ingredients and rub the lamb generously. Place the lamb in a bowl, cover with a plastic wrap and place in the fridge for an hour to marinate.

2. Stabilize the pit temperature to 250F (120C).

3. Smoke for 3 to 4 hours. Then check with an instant read thermometer. The target temperature is 145F (62C).

4. Check again after 20 minutes and remove from the pit once the meat reaches the temperature.

5. Rest for 30 minutes.

6. Slice and serve.

Chapter 4 Pork
Loin Ribs

(total cook time 3 hours 30 minutes to 4 hours)

Ingredients for 4 servings

The Meat

- Fresh loin ribs – 2, membrane removed (3-lb; 1.5kg)

The Fire

- Light your pit fire 1 hour prior to smoking

- Add wood 30 minutes prior to smoking

The Rub

- Dark brown sugar – 2 cups, loosely packed

- Kosher salt – ¾ cup

- Cayenne pepper – 1 tbsp.

- Mustard powder – 2 tbsp.

- Cumin – 1 tbsp.

Method

1. In a bowl, add the rub ingredients and mix well.

2. Apply rub to both sides of the rib racks. Allow to rest 45 minutes, uncovered.

3. Stabilize the pit temperature at 270F (132C). Place rib racks in the middle of the pit with tongs. To allow good airflow, leave at least a finger's width between rib racks.

4. Check rib racks after 3 hours 30 minutes by lifting them with tongs. Rib racks should flex with some separation of bark and meat. The target temperature is 270F (132C). Check with an instant read thermometer if needed.

5. Remove the rib racks once the target temperature is reached, up to 30 minutes later.

6. Rest for 20 minutes and serve.

SPARE RIBS

(TOTAL COOK TIME 4 TO 5 HOURS)

INGREDIENTS FOR 4 SERVINGS

The Meat

- Spare ribs – 2 (3.5-lb.; 1.6kg)

The Fire

- Light your pit fire 1 hour prior to smoking
- Add wood 30 minutes prior to smoking

The Rub

- Dark brown sugar – 2 cups
- Granulated sugar – 1 cup
- Kosher salt – ½ cup
- Cracked black pepper – ½ cup
- Cayenne pepper – 1 tbsp.
- Garlic pepper – 1 tbsp.
- Onion powder – 1 tbsp.
- Celery salt – 2 tsp.

Method

1. In a bowl, mix all the rub ingredients.
2. Apply rub to rib racks and rest uncovered for 45 minutes.

3. Stabilize the pit temperature at 250F (120C) and place the rib racks in the middle of the pit with tongs. For proper airflow, leave at least a finger's width between rib racks.

4. Check the racks for doneness after two hours. The target temperature is 250F (120C).

5. Check again after 2 more hours of cooking. Check with an instant read temperature. Rib racks should flex with some separation of bark and meat.

6. Once flex feels tender, remove the rib racks from the pit. After 30 minutes or 1 hour later.

7. Rest for 20 minutes and slice.

Pulled Pork Butt

(Total cook time 5 hours 30 minutes to 6 hours)

Ingredients for 10 to 12 servings

The Meat

- Pork butt – 1 (6-7 lb.; 2.7-3.2 kg)

THE FIRE

- Light your pit fire 1 hour prior to smoking

- Add wood 30 minutes prior to smoking

THE RUB

- Dark brown sugar – 2 cups

- Kosher salt – ½ cup

- Dry mustard powder – 5 tsp.

- Smoked paprika – 3 tsp.

- Onion powder – 1 ½ tsp.

- Garlic powder – 1 ½ tsp.

- Cayenne pepper – 1 tsp.

METHOD

1. In a bowl, add the rub ingredients and mix well.

2. Stabilize the pit temperature at 275F (135C). Place the pork butt in the middle of the pit with tongs.

3. Check the meat after 3 hours. The target temperature is 195F (90C). Check the temperature with an instant-read thermometer.

4. Once the pork butt has reached the target temperature (after almost 3 hours), remove from the pit.

5. No need to rest; slice and serve.

PORK BELLY

(TOTAL COOK TIME 1 HOUR 30 MINUTES)

INGREDIENTS FOR 4 SERVINGS

THE MEAT

- Square pork belly – 1 (1 -lb.; 450g), skin on

THE FIRE

- Light your pit fire 1 hour prior to smoking

- Add wood 30 minutes prior to smoking

THE RUB

- Dark brown sugar – 2 cups

- Granulated sugar – 1 cup

- Kosher salt – ½ cup

- Cracked black pepper – ½ cup

- Smoked paprika – 1 tbsp.

- Garlic powder – 1 tbsp.

- Onion – 1 tbsp.

METHOD

1. In a bowl, mix the rub ingredients.

2. Apply the rub generously to all sides of the pork belly.

3. Allow resting uncovered for 45 minutes before placing in the pit.

4. Stabilize the pit temperature at 310F (155C). Place the pork belly closer to the heat source with tongs.

5. Insert an instant-read thermometer into pork belly after 45 minutes. The target temperature is 160F (70C).

6. The pork belly will reach the target temperature after 30 minutes.

7. Remove from pit, slice and serve.

HAM

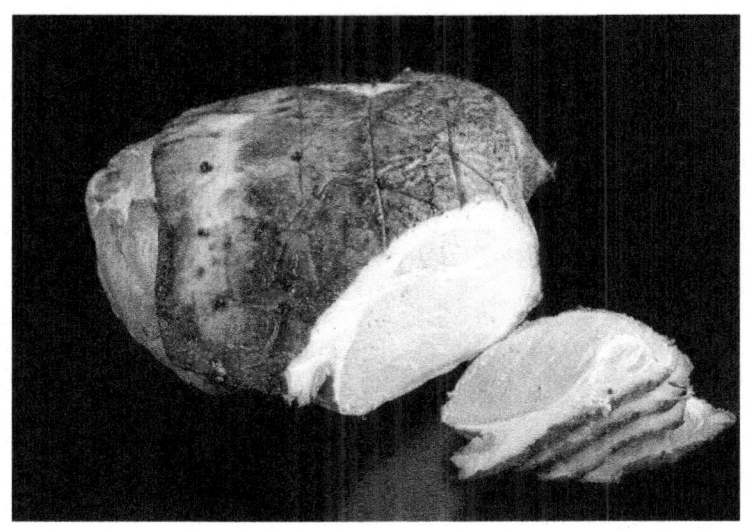

(TOTAL COOK TIME 3 TO 4 HOURS)

INGREDIENTS FOR 8 TO 10 SERVINGS

THE MEAT

- Uncured, bone-in half ham – 1 (7-lb.; 3.2kg)

THE FIRE

- Light your pit fire 1 hour prior to smoking
- Add wood 30 minutes prior to smoking

The Rub

- Dark brown sugar – 3 cups

- Kosher salt – ¼ cup

- Dry mustard powder – ¼ cup

- Garlic powder – 2 tbsp.

- Onion powder – 2 tbsp.

- Smoked paprika – 1 tsp.

Method

1. With a sharp knife, score ham in a criss-cross diagonal pattern (light incisions on the surface). Set aside.

2. In a bowl, mix the rub ingredients.

3. Stabilize your pit temperature at 300F (150C). Place the ham on the middle rack with tongs. Place the largest end toward the heat.

4. Check with an instant read thermometer after 2 hours. The target temperature is 150F (66C).

5. After 1 more hour, the ham will reach the target temperature. Remove it from the pit.

6. Allow to rest 40 minutes, uncover.

7. Slice and serve.

CHAPTER 5
POULTRY
TURKEY BREAST

(TOTAL COOK TIME 4 HOURS TO 4 HOURS 30 MINUTES)

INGREDIENTS FOR 6 TO 7 SERVINGS

THE MEAT

- Large turkey breasts – 2 (3- to 3¼-lb.; 1.5 to 1.6kg), skin removed

THE FIRE

- Light your pit fire 1 hour prior to smoking
- Add wood 30 minutes prior to smoking

THE RUB

- Light brown sugar – ¼ cup
- Paprika – 2 tbsp.
- Butcher's grind black pepper – 2 tsp.
- Kosher salt – 2 tsp.
- Garlic powder – 1 tsp.
- Onion powder – 1 tsp.
- Cayenne pepper – ½ tsp.
- Ground sage – ½ tsp.
- Ground thyme – ½ tsp.

METHOD

1. In a bowl, combine rub ingredients and mix well.

2. Apply the rub all sides of the turkey breasts.

3. Allow the turkey breasts to rest, 45 minutes uncovered.

4. Stabilize the pit temperature at 250F (120C). Place turkey breasts in the center of the pit with tongs. Keep larger ends towards the fire.

5. Insert an instant read thermometer after 3 hours to check the progress. The target temperature is 160F (70C).

6. After 1 hour to 1 hour,30 minutes more cooking the turkey breasts will reach the target temperature.

7. Remove from pit and rest for 30 minutes.

8. Slice and serve.

Smoked Quail

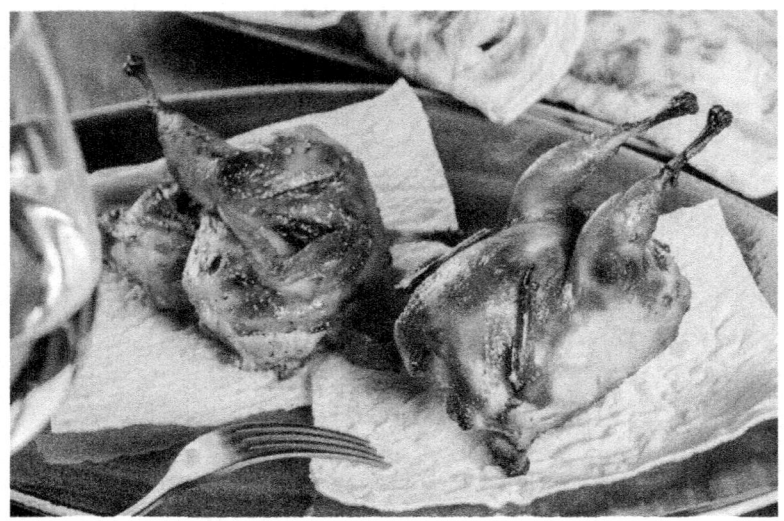

(TOTAL COOK TIME 45 MINUTES)

INGREDIENTS FOR 4 SERVINGS

THE MEAT

- Spatchcocked quail - 8 (½-lb.; 225g)

THE FIRE

- Light your pit fire 1 hour prior to smoking
- Add wood 30 minutes prior to smoking

The Rub

- Kosher salt – 1 cup

- Cracked black pepper – ¼ cup

- Ground sage – 1 tsp.

- Cayenne pepper – 1 tsp.

- Jalapeno peppers – 8 medium, chopped

- Crisp, tart apples – 2, chopped

Method

1. Except for the jalapeno and apples, combine the other rub ingredients in a bowl.

2. Rub the mixture on the quails and cover cavities.

3. Place several apple slices and jalapeno halves into the cavity of each quail.

4. With skewers, enclose the quails with apples and jalapenos inside.

5. Allow resting 45 minutes uncovered before placing in the pit.

6. Stabilize the pit temperature at 240F (115C). Place the quails in the middle of the pit with tongs.

7. After 45 minutes, test quail by gently tugging downward at thigh.

8. If legs get separate from the body, remove the quail and allow to rest uncover for 10 minutes and serve.

Chicken Wings

(Total Cook Time 1 Hour and 30 Minutes)

Ingredients for 3 Servings

- Chicken wings: 12 (3- to 4-oz.; 85 to 110g)

The Fire

- Light your pit fire 1 hour prior to smoking
- Add wood 30 minutes prior to smoking

The Rub

- Garlic powder – 1 tbsp.

- Cayenne pepper – 3 tsp.

- Onion powder – 2 tsp.

- Dry thyme – 2 tsp.

- Dry parsley flakes – 2 tsp.

- Granulated sugar – 2 tsp.

- Salt – 2 tsp.

- Paprika – 2 tsp.

- Ground allspice – 1 tsp.

- Ground black pepper – ½ tsp.

- Crushed red pepper flakes – ½ tsp.

- Ground nutmeg – ½ tsp.

- Ground cinnamon – ¼ tsp.

Method

1. In a bowl, mix all the rub ingredients.

2. In a large zipper-lock plastic bag, place the rub and wings.

3. Close the bag and shake to mix. Keep the bag in the refrigerator overnight.

4. Remove the bag 30 minutes before place the meat in the pit.

5. Stabilize the pit temperature at 250F (120C). Place the chicken in the middle of the pit with tongs.

6. Check the chicken after 1 hour for doneness by pressing fingers to the meatiest part of the each wing. Meat should fill firm and when it is fully cooked, it should not have any elasticity.

7. The chicken wings will be cooked after 30 more minutes of cooking.

8. Remove from the pit, rest for 10 minutes and serve.

Whole Chicken

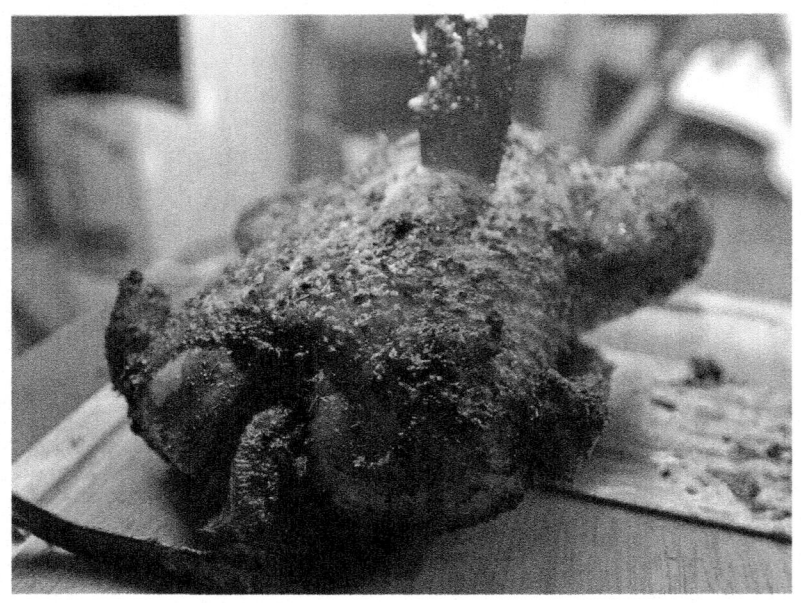

(TOTAL COOK TIME 4 HOURS 30 MINUTES TO 5 HOURS)

INGREDIENTS FOR 3 TO 4 SERVINGS

THE MEAT

- Whole chicken - 1 (3- to 6-lb.; 1.5 to 2.7kg)

THE SMOKE

- Light your pit fire 1 hour prior to smoking
- Add wood 30 minutes prior to smoking

THE RUB

- Kosher salt – ½ cup
- Light brown sugar – ½ cup
- Cracked black pepper – ¼ cup
- Paprika – 1 tsp.
- Cumin – 1 tsp.
- Cayenne pepper – 1 tsp.
- Ground sage – ½ tsp.
- Ground thyme – ½ tsp.
- Garlic – 3 cloves, minced
- Butter – 4 slices (1/4 inch thick)
- Lemon -1, cut into quarters

METHOD

1. Except for the lemon, butter, and garlic, mix all the other ingredients in a bowl.

2. Insert your fingers just above the cavity and make to pockets under the skin and above the breast meat.

3. Gently stuff 2 slices of butter and ½ of minced garlic into each pocket.

4. Place lemon quarters into the cavity.

5. Rub the chicken with rub mixture and place some inside the cavity. Allow resting for 25 minutes.

6. Bind the legs and thighs with strings so the chicken holds its shape.

7. Stabilize pit temperature at 260F (125C). Place the chicken in the middle of the pit and make sure cavity end faces the heat source.

8. Insert an instant read thermometer into the thickest part of the chicken after 3 hours 30 minutes. The target temperature is 165F (75C).

9. After another 1 to 1 hour 30 minutes of cooking, the chicken will reach the target temperature.

10. Remove the chicken from the pit and rest uncovered for 20 minutes.

11. Cut the chicken and serve.

CHICKEN THIGHS

(TOTAL COOK TIME 2 HOURS 30 MINUTES TO 3 HOURS)

INGREDIENTS FOR 4 SERVINGS

THE MEAT

- 8 skin-on chicken thighs (3 lb.; 1.5kg)

THE FIRE

- Light your pit fire 1 hour prior to smoking
- Add wood 30 minutes prior to smoking

The Rub

- Kosher salt – 1 cup

- Cracked black pepper – 2 tbsp.

- Granulated sugar – 1 tbsp.

- Cayenne pepper – 1 tsp.

- Paprika – 1 tsp.

- Ground sage – ½ tsp.

- Ground thyme – ½ tsp.

- Extra virgin olive oil – 4 oz.

Method

1. Except for the olive oil, combine all the rub ingredients in a bowl.

2. Rub the chicken thighs with the rub.

3. Pour extra-virgin olive oil in a small bowl and set aside.

4. Rest the chicken thighs uncovered for 45 minutes.

5. Stabilize the pit temperature at 260F (125C). Place the chicken thighs with tongs in the middle of the pit; keep the skin-side up.

6. Brush the skin side with olive oil after 1 hour and flip the chicken thighs.

7. After 1 hour, flip chicken thighs again.

8. After 30 more minutes, insert an instant read thermometer into the chicken thigh to check the progress. The target temperature is 160F (70C).

9. After 30 more minutes, the chicken thighs will reach the target temperature. Remove them from the pit.

10. Rest for 10 minutes and serve.

CHAPTER 6 GAME

VENISON LOIN

(TOTAL COOK TIME 40 TO 50 MINUTES)

INGREDIENTS FOR 4 SERVINGS

THE MEAT

- Whole venison tenderloins – 2 (1 -lb.; 450g)

The Fire

- Light your pit fire 1 hour prior to smoking

- Add wood 30 minutes prior to smoking

The Rub

- Fresh sage – 1 bunch, divided

- Apple – 1, sliced

- Butter – 115 g (in a pan)

Method

1. Stabilize pit temperature at 250F(120C). Place the venison tenderloins in the middle of the pit with tongs. Keep the larger ends toward the fire.

2. Place the pan with butter in the pit to melt.

3. Dip the sage brush into the melted butter after 15 minutes and slap it onto each tenderloin.

4. Insert an instant read thermometer into the middle of each tenderloin after 20 minutes to check the progress. The target temperature is 135F (57C).

5. After 5 to 15 minutes of more cooking, the tenderloins will reach the target temperature. Apply more butter with the sage and then remove from the pit.

6. Allow to rest the tenderloins for 10 minutes and place the apple slices into the pit and smoke for 5 minutes.

7. Slice tenderloins in medallions and garnish with sage leaves and smoked apple slices.

BOAR RIBS

(TOTAL COOK TIME 3 HOURS 30 MINUTES TO 4 HOURS)

INGREDIENTS FOR 2 SERVINGS

THE MEAT

- Wild boar ribs – 1 rack (3-4.5 lb.; 1.5-2 kg)

THE FIRE

- Light your pit fire 1 hour prior to smoking

- Add wood 30 minutes prior to smoking

THE RUB

- Kosher salt – ¼ cup

- Butcher's grind black pepper – ¼ cup

- Light brown sugar – 1 tbsp.

- Cumin – 1 tbsp.

METHOD

1. In a bowl, mix the rub ingredients.

2. Apply the rub generously to all sides of the rib rack.

3. Rest uncovered for 45 minutes.

4. Stabilize pit temperature to 255F (123C). Place the rib rack into the middle of the pit with tongs.

5. After 3 hours, test the ribs for doneness by lifting them in middle of the rack with tongs. You can also use an instant read thermometer. The target temperature is 170F (77C).

6. After 30 minutes to 1 hour more cooking, the ribs should reach the target temperature.

7. Remove from the pit and rest for 10 minutes.

8. Cut and serve.

Bison Ribeye

(TOTAL COOK TIME 40 MINUTES)

INGREDIENTS FOR 2 SERVINGS

THE MEAT

- Bison ribeye steaks – 2 (10 oz.; 285 g)

THE FIRE

- Light your pit fire 1 hour prior to smoking
- Add wood 30 minutes prior to smoking

The Rub

- Kosher salt – 1 cup

- Butcher's grind black pepper – 1 cup

Method

1. In a bowl, mix the rub ingredients.

2. Rub the rub mixture liberally on both sides of the steaks.

3. Allow resting 45 minutes uncovered before placing into the pit.

4. Stabilize the pit temperature at 275F (135C). Place the steaks into the middle of the pit with tongs.

5. After 30 minutes, insert an instant read thermometer in the middle of the steak to check the progress. The target temperature is 275F (135C).

6. After 10 more minutes of cooking, the steaks should reach the target temperature.

7. Remove from the pit and place on the coals immediately.

8. Sear for 2 minutes per side, turning once.

9. Remove steaks from the coals and rest for 10 minutes before serving.

PHEASANT

(TOTAL COOK TIME 4 HOURS TO 4
HOURS 30 MINUTES)

INGREDIENTS FOR 4 SERVINGS

THE MEAT

- Whole pheasant – 1 large (2.5 - to 3- lb.; 1.1 to 1.5kg)

THE FIRE

- Light your pit fire 1 hour prior to smoking

- Add wood 30 minutes prior to smoking

THE BRINE

- Light brown sugar – ¼ cup

- Kosher salt – ¼ cup

- Warm water – 7 to 8 cups

THE RUB

- Light brown sugar – ¼ cup

- Dry sage – 1 tbsp.

- Cumin – ½ tbsp.

- Garlic powder – 1 tsp.

METHOD

1. Place a large pot over low heat. Add warm water, brown sugar and salt. Mix and melt. Set aside to cool.

2. In the pot, fully submerge the pheasant. Cover with a lid and keep in the refrigerator overnight.

3. Remove the pheasant from the refrigerator 1 hour before placing in the pit and pat dry.

4. Mix the rub ingredients in a bowl and rub the pheasant with rub mixture. Rest 30 minutes before placing in the pit.

5. Stabilize the pit temperature at 220(105C)F. Place the pheasant in the middle of the pit with tongs and keep the breast side up. Make sure cavity facing the fire.

6. Check with an instant read thermometer after 3 hours and 30 minutes. The target temperature is 160F (70C).

7. After 30 to 1 more hour of cooking, the pheasant will react the target temperature.

8. Remove from the pit and allow the pheasant to rest uncovered for 10 minutes.

9. Slice and serve.

ELK TENDERLOIN

(TOTAL COOK TIME 50 MINUTES TO
1 HOURS 30 MINUTES)

Ingredients for 8 servings

The Meat

- Elk loin – 1 (3.5 lb.; 1.6 kg)

The Fire

- Light your pit fire 1 hour prior to smoking
- Add wood 30 minutes prior to smoking

The Rub

- Kosher salt – ¼ cup
- Cracked black pepper – ¼ cup
- Granulated sugar – 1 tbsp.

Method

1. Pat dry the lion with a paper towel.
2. In a bowl, mix all the rub ingredients.
3. Liberally rub the strip loin with the rub and rest at room temperature for 45 minutes.
4. Stabilize the pit temperature at 285F (141C). Place the strip loin in the middle of the pit with tongs.

5. Insert an instant read thermometer into the strip loin to check the progress after 50 minutes. The target temperature is 285F.

6. After 30 minutes more cooking the strip loin will reach the target temperature.

7. Remove from the pit and rest uncovered for 10 minutes.

8. Slice and serve.

CONCLUSION

The book includes 25 smoked meat recipes comprising beef, lamb, pork, poultry, and game. If you want to just treat yourself with mouthwatering, perfectly cooked smoked meat or entertain family or friends, this book will provide everything you need.

P.S. Thank you for reading this book. If you've enjoyed this book, please don't shy, drop me a line, leave a review or both. I love reading reviews and your opinion is extremely important for me.

My Page on Amazon
amazon.com/author/garymercer

This disclaimer applies to any loss, damages or injury caused by the use and application, whether directly or indirectly, of any advice or information presented, whether for breach of contract, tort, negligence, personal injury, criminal intent, or under any other cause of action.

You agree to accept all risks of using the information presented inside this book.

You agree that by continuing to read this book, where appropriate and/or necessary, you shall consult a professional (including but not limited to your doctor, attorney, or financial advisor or such other advisor as needed) before using any of the suggested remedies, techniques, or information in this book.

CPSIA information can be obtained
at www.ICGtesting.com
Printed in the USA
LVOW03s1931201217
560368LV00016B/1393/P